I'm the Boss of My Body

I'm the Boss of My Body

Patricia Barden

Cataloguing-in-Publication
National Library of Australia
Canberra ACT 2600
PH: +61 2 6262 1458

National Library of Australia Cataloguing-in-Publication entry

Creator: Barden, Patricia Una, author.

Title: I'm the boss of my body/Patricia Una Barden ;
Amy Patricia Barden, editor;
Karen Jane Gibson, Illustrator

ISBN: 9780646931968 (paperback)

Subjects: Child abuse—Prevention—Handbooks, manuals, etc.
Bullying—Prevention—Handbooks, manuals, etc.
Children's rights—Australia.

Other Creators/Contributors:
Barden, Amy Patricia, editor.
Gibson, Karen Jane, illustrator.
Wordzworth.com, typesetters.

Dewey Number: 362.70994

Dedicated to Amy Barden, Karen Gibson and Chanelle Bransgrove for inspiring the creation of this book for children.

Every day in the safest way
I have the right to rest and play

When someone tries to harm me
I need to be the Boss and say
STOP!

If I am hurt
or I don't feel safe

I must tell someone!

Someone who can help me
Someone who will keep me safe

Authors note

During my career as an educator working with young children, the safety of children placed in my care has always been a priority.

I have been inspired by parents to create a story that can be read to very young children about the subject of bullying and child protection.

The story line will stimulate questions and help children to understand there is a difference between good and bad feelings, what is right and what is wrong, the importance of self-protection and asking for help when they are at risk of harm.

Ask children the question, 'what would you do if you need help?'

This book is a resource to be read to children and then for children to read themselves.

I hope the idea of 'I'm the Boss of my Body' will give children a voice, and that the person they turn to for help will have the strength and ability to advocate on their behalf to keep them safe.

Patricia Una Barden.

© Patricia Barden 2013.

www.ingramcontent.com/pod-product-compliance
Lightning Source LLC
Chambersburg PA
CBHW042146290426
44110CB00002B/126